Original title:
Ode to the Tropics

Copyright © 2025 Creative Arts Management OÜ
All rights reserved.

Author: Aurora Sinclair
ISBN HARDBACK: 978-1-80581-940-0
ISBN PAPERBACK: 978-1-80581-467-2
ISBN EBOOK: 978-1-80581-940-0

Woven Whispers from Above

In the sun, the coconuts scheme,
While parrots plot a fruity dream.
Palm trees dance in silly glee,
Waving like they're wild and free.

Lizards laugh with cheeky grins,
As the warm breeze plays violin.
Mangoes roll like playful kids,
Hiding secrets under their lids.

Tropical rain wears rubber shoes,
Playing hopscotch with the blues.
Splashing puddles, don't you see?
Nature's jesters, laughing spree!

Underneath the twinkling night,
Fireflies twinkle, oh so bright.
They jive and jangle, quite the sight,
In this land where fun takes flight.

A Tropical Duet of Sun and Sky

The sun sings high with a cheerful tone,
While clouds giggle and dance alone.
A parrot tries to steal the show,
But the monkey just won't let it go!

Bananas hang in a merry line,
Whispering secrets, oh so fine.
They swing about on vines so high,
While iguanas give a sly eye.

Coconut crabs in a race so bold,
Scuttling quickly, or so we're told.
With a wink and a daring dive,
They zoom past where the fish thrive.

At sunset's edge, the colors blend,
And every creature finds a friend.
In this land of laughter and cheer,
The tropics share their funny sphere!

Melodies of Mangoes

In the shade, where mangoes sway,
Keeling down, I laugh and play.
Juice drips like a wild stream,
Sticky fingers—what a dream!

Sipping sunbeams in a cup,
Mango madness, never up!
I dance with bees, a sweet parade,
In this fruit-filled escapade!

Twilight on Turquoise Waters

Twilight giggles on the shore,
Surfboards dance, and seagulls soar.
A crab performs a silly jig,
Eyelids closing, belly big!

Laughing waves with frothy glee,
Turtle races, oh so free!
Sunset's glow, a goldfish ball,
Yet my flip-flop takes a fall!

Beneath the Bali Banyan

Beneath the tree with tangled roots,
I meet a frog in polka boots.
He croaks a tune, so very fine,
And hops to steal my last fried pine!

Swaying breezes, whispers tease,
Lizards plotting up the trees.
I join the dance with twirl and spin,
Under the stars, let the fun begin!

Paradise's Heartbeat

A coconut rolls like a bowling ball,
I trip and tumble—oh, how I fall!
Palm trees snicker as I fumble,
What a comedy, it's quite a jumble!

Dancing parrots steal the show,
Brighten my day with vibrant glow.
In this paradise where laughter rings,
Life's a circus, oh the joy it brings!

Flames of the Setting Sun

The sun dips low, a fiery ball,
It casts a glow on everything small.
The crabs are dancing with silly cheer,
They pinch and prance, oh how they leer.

A parrot squawks in vibrant hues,
Demanding snacks, maybe some booze.
The palm trees sway like they've had a drink,
While tourists ponder, 'What do we think?'

Serene Shores and Hidden Paths

The beach is a stage for a comedy show,
With sandcastles toppled by waves in tow.
A sunburned tourist, a sight to see,
Wonders why skin and sunscreen don't agree.

Seagulls swoop down for a snack or two,
Stealing fries from that silly review.
Hidden paths winding, long and absurd,
Lead to no treasure, just that blushing bird.

The Allure of Tropical Night

When night falls soft, the fun runs rife,
The fireflies flirt, 'tis a magical life.
A lizard with swagger struts like a king,
While folks on the dance floor give it a swing.

Beach bonfires crackle with spirit and glee,
Ghost stories told with a touch of brie.
The moon gives a wink, takes joy in the scene,
As locals gossip on the latest cuisine.

Drenched Dreams in Dappled Light

Under the shade, a hammock does swing,
Splashes of juice and the laughter they bring.
A monkey swings by with a coconut grin,
While sunbathers shout, 'Hey, don't let me in!'

The drizzle arrives with a playful tease,
Turning sunbathers to frantic flurries.
With puddles around, the kids make their splash,
As laughter echoes in this vibrant bash.

Sun-Drenched Serenades

In the sun, I spilled my drink,
Lemonade or was it pink?
Sipped too fast and made a splash,
Now my shirt's a sticky mash.

Flip-flops flapping, off I go,
Tripping lightly, nice and slow.
Caught a crab that danced on sand,
Soon he led a conga band.

Dance of the Tropical Breezes

Waves are whispering tales to me,
About the fish that swim with glee.
Caught a glimpse of a crab in style,
He winked, then danced a twisted mile.

Coconuts roll with giddy cheer,
While parrots squawk their tales so clear.
A breeze tickles my sunburned nose,
And laughter blooms among the throes.

Secrets Among the Palms

Beneath the palms, I spy a hat,
Left behind by some sunburnt brat.
A monkey swings, then grins so wide,
Snatches snacks with jungle pride.

Secrets rustle in the leaves,
Whispers shared among the thieves.
Lemons giggle from their trees,
As I dance with the humming bees.

Rhythms of the Rainforest Heart

Raindrops tap a rhythm wild,
I jump and twirl like a gleeful child.
Splashing puddles fill my shoes,
Now my toes have caught the blues.

Frogs croak verses, quite absurd,
As sloths sing the silliest word.
The jungle boogies, oh what fun,
With every laugh, I feel more spun.

Stars Over Paradise

Beneath the moon so bright, it peeks,
The monkeys chatter, share their freaks,
Palm trees sway to the rhythm's prank,
While seashells gossip on the sandbank.

The stars dance like they're at a ball,
A coconut drops with a comical fall,
Turtles in tuxedos waddle by,
And crabs scuttle with a cheeky sigh.

Whispers of the Warm Winds

Warm winds tease with a playful caress,
They rustle leaves, create a mess,
A parrot declares the weather fine,
Then steals a fruit, such a sly line!

Laughter floats on tropical breath,
As beachgoers dodge a playful theft,
The sun, a jester in the sky,
Winks at us as the clouds drift by.

Emerald Canopy Melodies

The treetops hum a jolly tune,
Where sloths are slow, and owls are croon,
Lizards leap with a wink and a grin,
As butterflies dance on a whimsy spin.

Each rustle brings a giggling breeze,
While iguanas wear their spiky ease,
A toucan laughs with vibrant flair,
As if nature's joke hangs in the air.

Lullabies of the Lush

In the heart of green, where giggles grow,
The river chuckles with a gentle flow,
Frogs croak solos, quite the delight,
While fireflies twinkle in the night.

The jungle hums a soothing jest,
As bats swoop low, never to rest,
A chorus of life, with whimsy we play,
In the lush embrace, we laugh all day.

Sounds of Cycle and Change

The parrot squawks with flair,
As monkeys swing with glee.
A toucan in a bright green chair,
    Still can't find his keys!

The sun beats down like a drum,
    While lizards dance on rocks.
Coconuts go thud, then hum,
And steal my summer socks!

With every breeze, a new surprise,
    A crab in slippers struts.
Who knew the trees had such wise eyes,
    As they keep track of nuts?

Fish below with silly grins,
Dive to claim the crown.
In this land of earthy whims,
Who could possibly frown?

Sunkissed Reflections on Water

Glances on the shimmering lake,
Where frogs wear fancy hats.
The fish are keen to take a break,
And chat about old cats.

Bees buzz by with gossip sweet,
While ducks do silly walks.
The sun's a jester on his seat,
Laughing at their squawks.

Reflections dance, all out of line,
As turtles play charades.
The flamingos sip some wine,
Dreaming up escapades!

With every splash, giggles arise,
As ripples share their jokes.
The water hosts a wild disguise,
Where even fish wear cloaks!

Exotic Ventures in Vibrant Greens

In jungles where the laughter flies,
The vines swing low and high.
A sloth in shades, oh what a prize,
Dreams of a sweet pie!

The parrots play a guessing game,
With fruit that looks like sticks.
In color bursts, there's no shame,
Plus bonus jungle tricks!

A lizard in a top hat prances,
Judging all the flair.
He challenges the monkeys' dances,
To feats beyond compare!

Among the blooms and funny smells,
The air pulsates with cheer.
In every twist, a story tells,
Of life both wild and dear.

The Lush Land's Lullaby

The palms sway slow, a gentle sigh,
As crickets play their tunes.
A frog croaks softly, oh my my,
Underneath the moon's balloons.

The night brings whispers, warm and sweet,
With fireflies as the stars.
While chameleons softly greet,
And claim the best guitars!

Beneath the leaves, the stories rustle,
Of lovers lost in cheer.
The softest sounds, a cozy bustle,
Only the brave can hear.

On slumbering shores, the dreams take flight,
In this land of plays and pranks.
Where laughter wraps the world at night,
In nature's merry ranks!

Salty Sea Spray Revelry

A seagull steals my sandwich,
With a caw and a cheeky grin.
I wave my flippered hand,
As waves of laughter begin.

Sunburnt tourists stumble,
Chasing kites that are too bold.
Sandbags weigh down their sandy toes,
But still, their joy won't fold.

Beach attire from a circus,
Flamingos and polka dots.
Sandy drips on picnic tables,
In laughter, they're all caught.

The ocean's got some rhythm,
As crabs dance to the beat.
With every splash and giggle,
Life here feels quite sweet.

Cascading Colors of Paradise

Tropical drinks are swirling,
With colors bright and loud.
Fruits piled high like mountains,
In a fruity, funny crowd.

Lemons wear the frowniest frowns,
As pineapples breakdance near.
Kiwi and mango bicker,
While we all lend an ear.

Sunsets paint the skies in jest,
As clouds join in the play.
Banana peels and laughter rise,
In this cheerful cabaret.

The rainbow's on vacation,
At our coastal, quirky show.
Each sip's a task of daring,
As fun and colors flow.

Elysian Gardens Beneath the Sun

In gardens of odd flowers,
Bouncing blooms all around.
Tulips gossip with daisies,
As bees join the sound.

Laughter springs from cacti,
As they tell a prickly joke.
Mushrooms giggle in corners,
Underneath the sun's cloak.

Sun hats dance on berry bushes,
Chasing butterflies in play.
In this wild, blooming circus,
Nature laughs all day.

Petunias wear sunglasses,
While daisies take a dip.
In these funny green pastures,
Life's a joyous trip.

Coral Dreams and Coastal Hues

Coral reefs wear shrimp as hats,
As fish parade in sparkles.
Octopuses are suddenly shy,
In colorful, wavy circles.

Starfish play hopscotch 'round rocks,
While turtles ponder what's next.
Bubbles rise with silly secrets,
In this underwater text.

A dolphin's dancing laughter,
Echoes through the bright blue.
Seahorses trot like dancers,
In their sparkling, fun crew.

The tide writes tales in whispers,
As gulls giggle overhead.
In this world of coral colors,
Joy and laughter are widespread.

Twinkling Stars Over Tropical Dreams

Beneath the stars, the crabs do dance,
They pinch my toes, such a funny chance.
While coconuts fall, I raise my cup,
To laughter and joy, we lift it up.

The moonlight plays, a silly game,
As iguanas strut, they're quite the fame.
With bright birds chirping in the night air,
Who knew the tropics could be this rare?

Pineapples roll, on the sandy beach,
They giggle away, just out of reach.
I chase them 'round, a merry old sight,
In tropical bliss, all feels just right.

As I nap in the sun, a wave splashes high,
A friendly dolphin gives me a sly eye.
Twinkling stars wink, as I dream of fun,
In this silly world, where laughter's won.

Threads of Misted Memories

In misty morn, the toucans call,
With beaks so bright, they stand so tall.
Memories linger like sweet, ripe fruit,
Tasting each moment like a juicy loot.

Banana peels slip, it's quite the show,
As monkeys swing, in a joyful flow.
Between the trees, they chatter and tease,
Leftovers dance in the warm, soft breeze.

A parrot squawks with comedic flair,
It mimics my laugh, does it with care.
Each twist of fate, a funny jest,
In the tropical realm, I'm feeling blessed.

As night descends, the fireflies blink,
Lighting up giggles, what do you think?
Threads of laughter weave through the air,
In this playful paradise, we forget our care.

The Flavor of Sunlit Days

Juicy mangoes drip, a sweet delight,
Sunlit days stretch 'til late in the night.
With laughter and whispers, the wind plays near,
Fruits of the tropics, bring us good cheer.

Coconuts grin, wearing silly hats,
While playful iguanas chase after cats.
Each bite of the sun, bursting with zest,
Laughter and sunshine, oh what a fest!

Silly toucans hop, with colors galore,
They poke fun at us, who could ask for more?
The flavor of days soaked in warmth and play,
In this bright world, we smile all day.

As the sun dips low, horizons ablaze,
We toast to the fun of these sunlit days.
With coconut drinks, and laughter so wide,
In the flavor of joy, we forever abide.

Rivers of Rhythm in Tropic Lands

In rivers bright, the fish do prance,
With scales that shimmer, they lead the dance.
Their splashes echo a cheeky beat,
As I wiggle my toes in the sun's warm seat.

Palms sway gently, in a whimsical breeze,
Laughter spills out from the lush green leaves.
A turtle floats by, wearing a grin,
In this fun paradise, let the games begin!

Maracas clink as the kiddos play,
Creating a rhythm that lights up the day.
Swaying to sounds of a carefree tune,
Under the rays of the silly, bright moon.

With coconuts rolling, and laughter so bold,
In tropical lands, where tales are untold.
Rivers of rhythm, where joy knows no end,
In this vibrant world, each day we'll spend.

Heartbeats of the Hidden Jungle

In leafy green, where monkeys swing,
The toucans boast, and parrots sing.
Watch out for vines that tickle your nose,
A jungle gym where laughter grows.

With every rustle, a giggle's found,
Sloths dance slowly, the clumsiest sound.
The jaguar jokes, with a mischievous stare,
"I can't catch you, but do I care?"

Lemurs prance in oversized shoes,
Playing tag while sipping their juice.
Ants throw a party, all dressed in black,
But trip over crumbs, now that's a hack!

The jungle breathes a cheeky delight,
Where even the shadows play peek-a-boo at night.
Join the fun with a wild, silly dance,
In nature's play, oh, what a chance!

Dappled Sunlight and Whispered Secrets

Beneath the leaves where sunbeams play,
A chameleon sips his coffee in sway.
Frogs croak tales of unending bliss,
While bees buzz loudly, not one to miss.

A shy sloth drops a nut with a thud,
It rolls away like a tiny flood.
The parakeets squawk with gossip galore,
As they gossip 'bout the iguana next door.

Sunlight dapples, it tickles the ground,
Where lizards lounge without making a sound.
Tickled by rays, the world sparkles bright,
As chubby little critters join the light.

Secretly giggling, the breeze plays a tune,
As raccoons dance under a big, silly moon.
The tropics hum with laughter and cheer,
In each soft whisper, more fun is near!

Palm Leaf Parables

Palm leaves sway with cheeky flair,
Sharing secrets in the tropical air.
The coconut falls, oh what a hit!
Is it a snack or a cheeky skit?

Crabs wear hats made of seashells bright,
Boasting of journeys on a starry night.
Their little dance brings giggles galore,
As they snap their claws and waddle some more.

Lush green tales spin 'round the bend,
With iguanas as judges and frogs as friends.
Each palm leaf holds a story or two,
Of fanciful dreams and laughter anew.

The sun dips low, the colors collide,
As party animals join in with pride.
Under palm trees, they're a silly crew,
In the wilderness, wild fun ensues!

The Tides' Timeless Tales

Waves crash in with a bubbly bounce,
The crabs in their shells, they twist and flounce.
Fish swim by wearing goofy grins,
Laughing along as the day begins.

The ocean whispers secrets untold,
While dolphins jive, brave and bold.
A whale's solo makes the beach sway,
As seashells conspire to dance and play.

The tides roll back, revealing the sand,
Where sandcastles stand, but not as planned.
Kids chase crabs in a raucous spree,
Turning the beach to a comedy.

Sunset chuckles as the day wears thin,
Stars peek out, ready to join in.
In tides' embrace, tales swirl and spin,
Forever captured: where giggles begin!

The Soothing Warmth of the Tropics

The sun shines bright on my stuffy hat,
Sweating like a pig, isn't that where it's at?
Pineapple dances with a rhythm so fine,
While mangoes just giggle, sipping on brine.

Flip-flops are squeaking on the hot, sandy shore,
Each step feels like stepping on cookies galore.
The palm trees wave with an overdone flair,
I think they're just jealous of my beachy hair.

Radiant Echoes Amongst the Trees

Swinging like a monkey, I lost my cool,
Chased by a parrot, my own feathered fool.
The toucans chuckle from high up above,
While I'm flailing about, not one speck of love.

Sunbeams filter through with a playful intent,
I squint my eyes hard, but no messages sent.
Laughter echoes back in this colorful dome,
As I try to decide if I'm lost or at home.

Quiet Reflections in Lush Gardens

In a garden so bright with flowers galore,
I found a snail dancing, what's he dancing for?
A butterfly flits by, with style and grace,
While I'm stuck in the mud—might need a new place.

The lilies are laughing, they've bloomed like mad,
Trying to tease me, but isn't it sad?
I'm here with the bees, who buzz with delight,
As I ponder my life choices, deep in this plight.

Harvest of Heavenly Hues

Fruits in the sun, oh what a sight!
I just dodged a papaya in mid-flight.
Beneath the banana trees, the laughter grows,
As I fumble with mangoes, striking a pose.

Coconuts rolling like they know the score,
I'm dodging, I'm weaving, then fall to the floor.
A harvest so tempting, it's all such a tease,
But I'll just embrace it with laughs and some cheese.

Sparkling Horizons at Dusk

In the sky, colors play,
A parrot steals my drink today.
Laughter echoes on the breeze,
A coconut drops with such a tease.

Flip-flops dance on sandy ground,
Where crabs scuttle all around.
The sun winks, it's time to cheer,
While seagulls compete for my fries here.

Luminous Legends of the Lagoon

Frogs croak tales of nights so grand,
A fish wears sunglasses, looking so tanned.
Mermaids gossip, hair in a knot,
But all I want is a cold coconut!

The lagoon sparkles, full of delight,
Where turtles race under moonlight.
I trip on waves, laugh with the breeze,
A splash! Look at me, wet as can be!

Fluidity Between Land and Sea

The sea tickles toes, a fun little game,
While land-lovers stare, it's such a shame.
I jump like a dolphin, try a big splash,
But land's my true calling: a sandwich I'd stash.

Sandcastles crumble beneath my might,
As waves giggle softly, what a sight!
Shells tell secrets, whisper and tease,
But all I hear is my hunger's wheeze.

Enchanted Isles of Memory

On an isle where pineapples grow,
I found a treasure, a stolen taco,
With rustling leaves, I join the parade,
As iguanas strut, this masquerade.

In sunsets of orange, the laughter unfolds,
Fighting with gulls for myths that they hold.
With memory made in bright, silly hues,
I leave with a smile, wet socks, and good views.

Plays of Light on Sandy Shores

Sunbeams dance on golden grains,
Kids giggle, running from waves' chains.
Seagulls squawk with playful glee,
While crabs shuffle, doing the shimmy!

Buckets spill with castles high,
While sunscreen turns the boy spry.
Sandcastles collapse, oh what a sight,
Yet laughter rises, pure delight!

Footprints vanish with the tide,
Tides tease back, oh, how they slide!
Beach balls soar, a colorful show,
And flip-flops race, to and fro.

Under the sun, a glorious game,
With each splash, a laugh to claim.
As the sun dips down with flair,
The night whispers, 'Don't you dare!'

Serpentining Paths Through Paradise

Paths twist like a dancer's legs,
Winding through the forest pegs.
Chameleons change with a wink,
As monkeys swing and do a blink!

Lush leaves hide a sneaky frog,
Croaking jokes, a comic hog.
Butterflies flutter, full of sass,
While trolls find shade, quite a pass!

Snakes slither with a charming twist,
A line of laughter, can't resist.
Bamboo shoots just love to jest,
While a parrot gives it a rest.

In this maze where fun ignites,
Every turn brings pure delights.
With giggles echoing, off we trot,
Life's a game, just like we thought!

Frames of Foliage and Light

Through the leaves, sunbeams peek,
Laughter echoes in chic technique.
Monkeys play in leafy dorms,
Jokes and giggles become their norms.

Palm trees sway with all their might,
Dancing shadows, pure delight.
Coconuts drop like comical bombs,
As youngsters weave through green balms.

Foliage thick with laughter's scent,
Nature's art, a funny event.
Chirping birds sing silly tunes,
A symphony beneath the moon.

In this haven where we get lost,
Every corner holds a cost.
With joy framed by nature's light,
Life's a show, oh what a sight!

Clouds Weaving Paradise Dreams

Clouds float like cotton candy dreams,
Tickling the sun's radiant beams.
Whales dive for jokes in the sea,
While dolphins giggle, "Look at me!"

Raindrops tap, a funny tune,
Chasing puddles, around we swoon.
Rainbow arcs, a silly smile,
Like nature dressed up in style.

Storms roll in with thunderous laughs,
Painting skies with playful crafts.
Lightening dances, zap and zing,
While wind plays hide-and-seek, oh, sing!

In dreams woven through the breeze,
We find joy among the trees.
With clouds above in playful schemes,
Life is funny, or so it seems!

The Song of the Salt Air

The seagulls squawk, a funny tune,
They steal your fries; oh, what a boon!
Waves crash down with a silly splash,
In salty dance, all worries dash.

Beach umbrellas sway, a colorful sight,
Sandy toes wiggle with pure delight.
A crab in a hat scuttles by fast,
While sunbathers wonder how long they'll last.

Coconuts and Moonlight

Under moonlight, coconuts dream,
Rolling gently, it's quite the scheme.
One coconut grins, ready to drop,
"Catch me if you can," it says with a hop!

The beach bonfire flickers with cheer,
As locals dance, sipping cold beer.
A monkey swings down with a banana in tow,
"Join the luau!" he chirps, stealing the show!

Mongooses in the Moonlight

Mongooses prance with their furry tails,
Sneaking around with exaggerated fails.
They tiptoe softly, then burst into play,
Chasing shadows until it's day.

One takes a dive, a splash on the sand,
Another just tripped—oh, isn't it grand?
They giggle and wiggle beneath the night sky,
Crafty little creatures, oh my, oh my!

The Caress of Ocean Breezes

Ocean breezes tease your hair,
Tickling your nose without a care.
A beach ball bounces, then runs away,
Chasing it down means starting to play!

Laughter erupts as waves play tricks,
Splashing sunbathers, oh what a mix!
The breeze whispers secrets, both soft and light,
While flip-flops scamper out of sight.

Harmonies of Ocean and Earth

Waves laugh at the shore's embrace,
Seagulls dance in a tricky chase.
Palm trees sway, with a gentle tease,
While crabs plot their little frenzies.

Coral reefs wear their bright attire,
Fish with flair, a true aquatic choir.
Sandcastles rise, then swiftly fall,
As kids giggle and give it their all.

Sunsets drip in colors so wild,
Nature's stage, forever beguiled.
With flip-flops lost, the beach a riot,
Who knew the shore could be a diet?

A coconut falls with a hefty thud,
While tourists applaud with heart and blood.
In this land where the sun loves to play,
Laughter reigns, come join the ballet!

Canvases of Nature's Palette

Painted skies, a tangerine burst,
Butterflies flit, in flowered thirst.
Bamboo sways, a ticklish affair,
In this joyful land, we lose our care.

The parrots squawk in vivid cheer,
Sipping nectar, they draw near.
Sunflowers grinning, a golden mess,
Nature's giggles in bright excess.

An iguana dressed in emerald green,
Stumbles on branches, a sight unseen.
Mangoes drop with a juicy thump,
While monkeys join in with their wild jump.

The crickets chirp a silly tune,
Bats dance under the smiling moon.
With every brush stroke, there's laughter so rich,
Mother Nature's an artist; oh, what a stitch!

Nature's Rhapsody in Bloom

Flowers giggle in a colorful spree,
Dancing petals, oh, can't you see?
Buzzing bees wear little hats proud,
Humming tunes, forming a crowd.

Drifting scents on the playful breeze,
Stir up memories with the greatest of ease.
A butterfly lands with a sassy flair,
Tickling the leaves, what a grand affair!

The sun yawns, stretching wide with glee,
While ants march like a quirky army.
Raindrops dress the grass in bling,
In this rhapsody, hear nature sing!

With laughter bubbling like a brook,
Every flower blooms, every tree shakes a hook.
Nature's comedy, wild and free,
In each petal's secret, there's joy to see!

Velvet Nights and Colorful Days

Stars twinkle like they're in a play,
On velvet nights, oh, what a display!
Crickets serenade with their best notes,
Swapping jokes with the goats on the moats.

Sunrise paints with a brush so bold,
Colors spill like stories untold.
A rooster crows with a theatrical flair,
Wake-up calls that make you despair!

Fireflies glow, they're nature's bling,
Lighting paths while the night creatures sing.
A comical show, under the trees,
Where laughter mingles with the gentle breeze.

Daytime smiles with clouds that tease,
Nature's whims, as free as the breeze.
In this kingdom of jovial delight,
Let's dance through both day and night!

Swaying Palms and Starry Nights

Beneath the palms that dance with flair,
A coconut drops, if you dare!
Laughter echoes, the moon's a prank,
As we toast to friends with drinks in tank.

With every sway, the shadows bend,
A comical twist, our sleep, they fend.
We giggle at crabs that shuffle and roam,
In this paradise where all feel at home.

Twinkling stars like a ceiling of fun,
With each bright twinkle, the laughter's begun.
We'll sway with the tides, along the bright shore,
Finding too much joy, we just can't keep score.

So here's to nights that burst into song,
Where nothing feels right but still feels so wrong.
Swaying palms beckon a whimsical life,
Full of chuckles, love, and occasional strife.

The Secret Life of Rain

Raindrops giggle as they hit the ground,
In puddles they gather, such joy they've found.
They bounce in sync, a quirky parade,
While umbrellas flop, their plans delayed.

A cheeky cloud winks at the sun from afar,
In this wet tango, we laugh like we're stars.
With splashes of fun, they give water fights,
Each droplet a joke on these tropical nights.

Dancing in rain, we slip and glide,
Like toddlers at play, with no place to hide.
The plants start to chuckle, it seems they agree,
For life's just a tickle when rain's carefree.

So cheers to the rains that wash troubles away,
With a splash and a giggle, we'll dance and sway!
In this secret life, let's all take delight,
As rain drops its humor on us every night.

Jasmine and Journeys

With jasmine wafting in the warm breezes,
We're planning our trips through tropical eases.
A map in our hands with no sense of place,
And giggles galore in this scenic embrace.

The sun is our guide, the sand our dance floor,
As we trip over flip-flops, what fun to explore!
We'll ride on the waves, or more likely just float,
With laughter as loud as a lively old goat.

Adventures await on this path made of dreams,
Where nothing is real, or so it seems.
Each coconut tells tales of places to roam,
When all we need is the beach to call home.

In a world of jasmine, let's wander and sway,
With silly stories, we'll brighten the day.
For joy is the journey and laughter the key,
In this tropical bliss where we just want to be.

Vibrant Hues of the Dusk

As the sun takes a bow in the evening's embrace,
Painting the sky with colors we chase.
Crayons in hand, we scribble our dreams,
While sipping on coconuts, plotting our schemes.

The purple and gold, a comedic display,
As flamingos dance in their own quirky way.
They trip on the sand with their long, wobbly legs,
While laughter erupts, oh how our hearts beg!

The horizon is giggling, covered in hues,
With pink clouds above, sharing outrageous news.
Let's sketch out the future with hues that delight,
While shadows dance in the playful twilight.

So here's to the dusk that colors our nights,
Where every sunset's an excuse for delights.
In vibrant towns where the jokes never cease,
We'll celebrate life with laughter and peace.

Vibrant Petals in the Breeze

Colorful blooms dance in the light,
One flower begs, 'Come take a bite!'
Yet bees are buzzing with great delight,
While ants hold a wrestling night.

Butterflies in a swirling race,
Winging about in a silly chase.
'No flowers for you!' they leave no trace,
While daisies giggle, just in case.

The Soundtrack of Sundrenched Shores

Waves sing songs of splash and cheer,
As seagulls laugh, 'We own this pier!'
A crab sidesteps, with no fear,
While beach umbrellas spin like a reel.

Kids build castles, then dance in the sand,
'Oops, there goes our kingdom!' says a hand.
Sunbathers swapping sunscreen as planned,
While loud radios blare a strange band.

Nectar of the Night Blooms

Fireflies glow in a boisterous flight,
While frogs croak jokes in the pale moonlight.
A nocturnal party—Oh, what a sight!
As crickets chirp 'til dawn's first light.

Sweet scents waft from blooms so bold,
While bats play tag, much to behold.
With buzzing bees sharing tales retold,
The night reveals laughter that never grows old.

Echoes of the Lush Life

Comedy unfolds among the vines,
Parrots squawk jokes, performing lines.
Monkeys swing with goofy designs,
While sloths just take their good old times.

In the thick of fun, a snake does slide,
Wiggling, doing the 'slippery glide.'
The jaguar yawns, takes a wide-side,
"Are you not entertained?" it said with pride.

Dances of Deciduous Delight

In the forest, leaves twirl round,
Squirrels breakdance, so profound.
They wear hats, all feathered bright,
Nature's showgirls, pure delight.

Raindrops tap out a rhythm neat,
On a branch, a frog takes a seat.
He croaks a tune, so offbeat now,
Flipping his tongue—"Look at me, wow!"

A parrot squawks in disco tones,
Inviting all to shake their bones.
With every squawk, the trees all sway,
A boogie-woogie, come what may!

Finally, as night descends,
A moonlit rave, it never ends.
With branches swaying, all's a whirl,
In the tropics, life's a dance unfurl!

Songs from the Edge of the World

On the shore, the crabs perform,
In tiny hats, they break the norm.
With tiny claws, they sing along,
Creating melodies, oh so strong.

The seaweed sways, a groovy dance,
As fish pop up, they take a chance.
Their bubbles burst in giggling fits,
In this chorus, joy never quits.

Seagulls strut with their bold display,
They've got moves that steal the day.
With wings spread wide, they glide with grace,
In this concert, they take their place.

As twilight paints the sky in gold,
The creatures sing their tales retold.
From the beach, there's laughter wide,
At the world's edge, joy can't hide!

Veils of Vapor Rounding the Day

Morning mist, a playful tease,
Hides the flowers, but not the breeze.
Butterflies giggle, flit about,
Wearing dew drops as they sprout.

Clouds don't mind a cheeky grin,
Bouncing sunlight from within.
They puff out jokes, a floating jest,
In the azure, they feel blessed.

A parakeet juggles fruit with flair,
While the sun beams down everywhere.
Colors swirl like a carnival,
In this vapor, fun's the protocol!

As evening wraps the day with glee,
Stars peek through, a mystery.
With laughter sprinkled all around,
In the tropics, joy is found!

Flavors of the Exotic Ballet

In a market, spices chase the nose,
With dizzy colors, joy just grows.
Coconuts wobble with a laugh,
In this dance, they take a photograph.

Pineapples wear tutus, sprightly bright,
While mangoes pirouette in flight.
With a dash of lime, they all twirl round,
Making magic where fun is found.

Papayas join in, a structured leap,
As bananas peel off laughter deep.
A guava's giggle fills the air,
In this quirky show, nothing can compare.

At sunset's brush, the flavors blend,
In this ballet, joy has no end.
From fruits to spices, all in the fray,
In the tropics, life's a grand buffet!

Dance of the Hibiscus

Hibiscus in a floral dress,
Twisting in the playful breeze,
"Look at me!" it laughs with zest,
While butterflies dance with ease.

A bee buzzes in with flair,
Feeling fancy, quite the chap,
It sips nectar, unaware,
That it's stuck in a floral trap!

With petals soft and colors bright,
The flowers throw a grand ballet,
They shimmy, twirl, all day and night,
Making sunbeams want to sway.

So join the fun, you might just find,
That dancing blooms spread joy divine,
In tropical lands, so sweet and kind,
Where flowers frolic, and life does shine!

Echoes of the Rainforest

In the rainforest, the frogs are loud,
Croaking tunes like they're on stage,
They form a ribbit-ribbit crowd,
Each one vying for the next page.

Monkeys swing with cheeky cries,
Stealing snacks from careless birds,
They laugh and tease with darting eyes,
Creating mischief with their herds.

Parrots squawk a color show,
Chattering secrets, oh so grand,
While sloths take naps, moving slow,
Dreaming in their leafy land.

Echoes play in leafy halls,
Rainforest stories, wild and bold,
With every sound, the song enthralls,
Comedy woven in green and gold!

Coral Serenade

Beneath the waves, the fish do prance,
In coral homes that look surreal,
They wiggle and sway in a watery dance,
Chasing bubbles with bubbly zeal.

Starfish take the front-row seat,
While octopuses paint the sea,
With tentacles in rhythm, oh what a feat,
Their art's a splash of wild glee!

Clownfish jest, their laughter bright,
With a jig that's quite the sight,
"Who needs a stage?!" they croon with pride,
In this underwater gig, they'll ride.

With sea grass swaying, they find their way,
The coral world a stage of cheer,
In the sea's sweet symphony, they play,
A marine concert, loud and clear!

The Coconut's Embrace

Coconuts hang from palms so high,
Dreaming of vacations on the beach,
"Throw me down, I dare you!" they cry,
As if freedom's just within reach.

The breeze tickles, the tree sways,
A playful challenge to the sun,
"Catch me if you can!" it playfully bays,
As through the branches, it starts to run!

A curious kid walks on by,
With dreams of fresh coconut pie,
But first to dodge a drop from the sky,
"Watch out!" the palm trees laugh and sigh.

But when they land, it's all in smiles,
The hug of a coconut calms the spree,
With laughter ringing through the miles,
In every sip, a taste of glee!

Twilight's Carnival

As dusk unfolds a silly show,
The coconuts dance, putting on a glow.
The palm trees sway, with all their might,
While crickets chirp to the stars' delight.

With shades of pink, the skies turn bright,
A parrot laughs at the moon's funny sight.
"Look at me!" says a crab with flair,
As it scuttles away, giving a glare.

The fireflies twinkle, like little stars,
A coconut grin as it rolls from afar.
"Join the party!" they say with glee,
In this night circus, just you and me.

So grab a drink, and dance with the breeze,
As seagulls squawk, and dance on the seas.
Life in twilight is truly a blast,
With laughter and joy, let's forget the past.

Island Echoes

On this sandy shore, where the funny crabs play,
    Whispers of waves echo tales of the day.
    The sunbeams giggle, they tickle the sea,
    While mermaids snicker and sip iced tea.

The monkeys swing low, with bananas in hand,
    They caper and tumble, a wild, furry band.
    With each cheeky grin, and each silly joke,
They weather their worries, with laughter they soak.

The breeze takes a twirl, as a parrot requests,
    "Let's sing a tune, we are the very best!"
    So under the palms, we join in the song,
    In this island of echoes, where all go along.

With coconuts rolling, and laughter that spreads,
    The echoes of joy fill our hearts and our heads.
    As we dance with the dusk, oh, how time flies,
    In this world of mayhem, beneath tropical skies.

A Tapestry of Tides

The sea weaves stories, in shades of blue,
A tapestry of tides, where silliness grew.
Fish wear top hats and dance at the shore,
While gulls dive in laughter, demanding encore.

The waves clap their hands in a frothy delight,
They tumble and roll, playing hide and seek at night.
"Catch me if you can!" calls a sprightly wave,
As it leaps and twirls, so bold and brave.

Seashells gossip on a sunlit spree,
Exchanging tall tales, like gossiping trees.
"Oh, did you hear?" they muse and they giggle,
About a new fish that performs a jiggle.

As day surrenders to a frolicsome night,
The moon winks slyly at the glowing sight.
In this tapestry of tides, life sways and bends,
With humor stitched in, as the fun never ends.

Carved by Sun and Breeze

With laughter carved in the beams of the sun,
The beach comes alive, it's a whimsical run.
Children build castles, with moats full of dreams,
While sand tickles toes, and sunshine redeems.

The breeze blows in, wearing a feathered hat,
Whispers to the palm, "Hey, fancy that!"
They share silly secrets, like the best of friends,
While coconuts giggle, their humor transcends.

The sun makes a splash, in its golden parade,
Creating a dance floor, no need for charade.
Laughter echoes loud, as waves crash around,
In a world where joy and mischief abound.

So raise up your drinks, let's toast to the skies!
With warmth wrapping all, where humor never dies.
In the grip of the sun, with the breeze on our cheeks,
A dance of delight, in these tropical peaks.

Serengeti of the South Seas

In the ocean's wide embrace,
Where fish dance with a silly face,
The parrots squawk as they parade,
While crabs do cha-chas in the shade.

A turtle takes a leisurely stroll,
Donning shades, he plays the cool role,
The sun smiles down, a golden glee,
As dolphins giggle, wild and free.

Harmonies of Hibiscus and Breeze

The flowers sway, in pink and red,
While bees do a dance instead of dread,
A breeze comes by, with a whisk and twirl,
As nature spins and gives a whirl.

The coconut drinks are back in play,
With tiny umbrellas to brighten the day,
Laughter echoes through the palm trees,
As coconuts grin, 'Hey, lift with ease!'

Caravans of Color in the Air

Kites of colors fly up high,
While seagulls swoop and nudge the sky,
Each child points, with wide-eyed glee,
As candies rain from the mango tree.

The sun's a jester in this land,
Making shadows dance and play unplanned,
As monkeys steal a snack or two,
And giggles burst – oh, what a view!

Rhythmic Roars of the Rain

Raindrops fall with a funky beat,
As puddles echo the happy feet,
The frogs join in, a croaky choir,
Their jumping moves can never tire.

The clouds play peek-a-boo above,
Dancing silhouettes the skies shove,
With every splash, a chuckle breaks,
As laughter bursts, the earth awakes!

Whispers of the Emerald Isle

In green fields where the rabbits race,
A leprechaun forgot his place.
He spilled his pot, oh what a sight,
Gold coins rolling, what a fright!

The palm trees sway like dancers proud,
They laugh at clouds that form a crowd.
A monkey steals a drink or two,
While locals shout, "Hey! That's our brew!"

In the shade, the tourists gawk,
A crab scuttles, but they just talk.
Their sandals lost, bare feet they flaunt,
Chasing shadows that they all want!

With a coconut, a man will dare,
To juggle fruit without a care.
But as he slips, oh what a mess,
He yells, "This is my new job, I guess!"

Sun-Kissed Sorrows

A sunburnt nose, oh what a blight,
While sunscreen battles with daylight.
George forgot to apply it right,
Now he's Rudolph at the beach tonight!

The seagulls squawk with cheeky glee,
As they steal fries from a guy named Lee.
He waves his arms, makes quite a fuss,
While they munch happily on his lunch!

In the water, kids make a splash,
But lose their goggles in a crash.
They swim to find it, oh what joy,
Only to box with a floating toy!

As the sun dips low, it paints the sky,
A parrot mimics a passerby.
With laughter shared, they all unite,
Under the stars, it feels just right!

Lush Canopy Dreams

In jungles deep, the vines entwine,
A sloth takes ages, oh how divine!
He yawns and nods, then drifts away,
Living life at his own slow play!

The toucans gossip, brightly dressed,
While monkeys throw a wild fest.
Banana peels fly through the air,
As they laugh and dance without a care!

The tourists hike with wayward glee,
But trip on roots, oh woe is me!
They take a tumble, land on their backs,
Squealing with laughter as nature attacks!

Underneath the vibrant leaves,
The hidden frogs plot grand mischiefs.
They croak their jokes, each ribbit's a cheer,
In this goofy paradise, not one has fear!

Symphony of the Shore

At dawn's first light, the waves do sing,
As surfers try to catch the fling.
But wipeouts reign; it's quite a show,
As laughter echoes, we all know!

Sandy toes and ice cream dreams,
While icebergs bob in our melting schemes.
A dog steals treats from a beachside table,
As kids just stare, while soon they're able!

The locals play their ukuleles,
Singing tunes that lift all worries.
A crab joins in with rhythm fine,
Marching sideways, oh how they shine!

As twilight winks upon the shore,
Fireflies dance, demanding more.
With giggles shared beneath the stars,
It's good to be where joy's not far!

Echoes Through the Canopy

Swaying branches, birds collide,
A parrot squawks, his pride can't hide.
Laughter blooms among the trees,
While monkeys swing with silly ease.

A toucan sports a beak so wide,
He drops his fruit, oh what a glide!
The sloth rolls by, so slow, so cool,
While squirrels laugh, they think he's a fool.

The sun peeks through, a golden ray,
Reflecting on the ants at play.
With tiny hats, they march, oh dear,
A tiny parade, loud cheer to cheer!

Echoes dance in this vibrant place,
Nature's jesters, a funny face.
So come and join this wild affair,
In the tropical warmth, without a care.

Palm-Fringed Promenades

Strolling down the sandy lane,
Pineapples rolling, it's all in vain.
A coconut lands, what a surprise,
A beach ball substitute in disguise.

Sea turtles waddle with a grin,
While crabs play tag, they'll never win.
With sunglasses on, the seagulls stare,
At beachgoers lost in sun-filled despair.

There's laughter rising with the tide,
As beach umbrellas start to slide.
With every gust, a colorful flight,
As picnics scatter, what a sight!

Palm trees sway to a playful tune,
Swaying gently beneath the moon.
Join the fun where the sun stays bright,
For laughter waits in the warm daylight.

Phenomena of the Paradise Sky

Clouds that twist in forms unknown,
Like elephants or ice cream cones.
The sunset's glow, a painted smile,
Balloons take off, just for a while.

Stars pop out, it's a cosmic game,
A shooting star, oh what a fame!
A meteor shower rains down giggles,
As crickets dance, with silly wiggles.

Coconuts drop, creating thunder,
As night unveils its magical wonder.
Fireflies blink, a flickering show,
While the moon laughs in a silvery glow.

Under the sky, the antics unfold,
A story of ruckus, waiting to be told.
In this paradise, strange and bright,
Joy bounces high, all through the night.

Charms of the Caribbean Night

Under the stars, the nightlife sings,
With dancing waves and moonlit flings.
A conch shell plays a jazzy tune,
While crabs hold court under the moon.

One little fish in a tuxedo,
Dashes by with a perfect prelude.
He brings a party to the coral reefs,
With jellyfish twirls and shining leafs.

The scent of jerk spice fills the air,
With dancing goats who just don't care.
They prance and leap, a sight to see,
In this feast of nature, wild and free.

So grab your friends, let laughter flow,
In the Caribbean, where the fun will grow.
With charms galore and spirits bright,
Come and revel in this magical night.

Mango Moonlight and Coconut Stars

Mango dreams under moonlit skies,
Where coconuts giggle and dance with flies.
Laughter echoes through palm trees bright,
As crabs put on their shoes, oh what a sight!

Fruit punch spills, and we lose the game,
Tropical breezes, it's never the same.
Sipping on sunshine, oh what a thrill,
Keep your hat on tight—don't wander, don't chill!

Umbrellas twirl as the drinks get free,
See that crab making a dash for the sea?
A conch shell's shout, "You're invited, my friend!"
In this fruity fiesta, the fun never ends!

So here we are, laughing at fate,
Making fruit salads—large on a plate.
With mango moonlight and coconut stars,
We'll dance till the morning, 'neath a beach of guitars!

Paradise Found in Petals

Petals flutter like butterflies cheer,
Waving to sunbeams, "Hey, come over here!"
Bees in tuxedos buzz with delight,
As flowers gossip, oh what a sight!

Tropic tea parties with fruits on display,
Papayas in hats, and they're here to stay.
Watermelons joke with their juicy round grins,
Inviting the sun to come join in the spins!

A pineapple holds court, it's the king of the day,
While lemons and limes simply giggle and play.
The flowers all sway to the beat of the breeze,
While petals fall—nature's confetti, if you please!

Oh, paradise calls in this colorful show,
Where each bloom has secrets we're dying to know.
In this riot of color, let's celebrate cheer,
For in these bright petals, pure joy is near!

Sunkissed Shores of Serenity

Sunkissed shores where flip-flops roam,
Sandcastles rise like they're far from home.
Seagulls are diving for snacks in the sky,
While beach balls are bouncing, oh my, oh my!

Tanning lizards wear shades by the sea,
Chasing the waves, they sing joyfully.
Cool drinks in hand, we cheer to the fun,
As sand tickles toes, and we all try to run!

A crab in a hat thinks he's winning the race,
While sunburned tourists search for some shade space.
The sun plays peek-a-boo with waves that gleam,
In this sunny chaos, we're living the dream!

So bring on the laughter, the joy, and the cheer,
Where each rising wave sings magic in our ear.
Sunkissed shores whisper stories so fine,
With each splashy giggle, the world's truly divine!

Portraits of a Tropical Palette

Brush strokes of color on nature's canvas,
Where hidden smiley faces lighten the madness.
Tropical reds, and greens, oh so bright,
Where juggling pineapples chase off the night.

Coconut canvases line sandy routes,
Painting the skies in whimsical flouts.
Every hue dances, from dusk until dawn,
While guava giggles in its rosy lawn.

Pinky sunsets tiptoe along the horizon,
While monkeys chatter, their dance is a fusion.
In this art of laughter, colors collide,
Creating a world where joy can't hide!

So gather your palettes, the tools of delight,
Let each brush drip with joy, oh what a sight!
In portraits of charm, let's dance with the palm,
A tropical masterpiece—endlessly calm!

Swaying Silhouettes at Sunset

Under palm trees, we do a dance,
Swinging left, then right, oh what a chance!
The sun dips low with a wink and smile,
We trip on toes, laughing all the while.

Shadows stretch like silly clowns,
Belly laughs echo through ocean towns.
Coconut falls, a bump on the head,
But with a grin, we must be led!

Flip-flops fly, we lose our way,
Chasing sunsets at the end of the day.
Swaying silhouettes, a fantastic sight,
With giggles that dance into the night.

So let's sway with joy, don't be a bore,
In the tropic's flair, forever explore!
Our laughter rings like the ocean's roar,
At sunset's edge, who could ask for more?

The Tropics' Tender Embrace

Beneath the sun's warm, cheeky glow,
A high-five from a breeze, soft and slow.
Bananas giggle as they grow,
While we attempt our limbo flow.

A toucan boasts a silly beak,
With a feathered hat, it's quite unique.
Mangoes roll, our fruit parade,
We stumble and trip, but never fade.

Coconuts fall with a plop and a thud,
We laugh and dodge like we're in a flood.
With smiles so big and hearts so light,
The tropics steal our breath each night.

In hugs of warmth, we find our place,
As laughter fills the sunlit space.
So join the fun, don't hesitate,
In the tender arms of tropical fate.

Tropical Trinkets of Nature

Jellybeans hang from leafy trees,
While pineapple chairs invite with ease.
Crab with a hat tips its claw,
Winks at us with a little jaw.

Seashells whisper secrets to the sand,
While starfish giggle, hand in hand.
A parrot squawks, a cheeky tease,
As we dance around like buzzing bees.

The sun wears shades, strutting with flair,
While flowers bloom everywhere.
A smoothie spill, a slippery sight,
We laugh and play 'til the fall of night.

With trinkets of nature, quite absurd,
The tropics sing in a joyous word.
Join the fun, don't be a bore,
In this wild world, there's always more!

Celestial Skies

Up above, the stars play tag,
While clouds wear hats, oh what a brag!
The moon peeks in with a cheeky grin,
Inviting all to join the din.

Comets zoom with a joyful cheer,
Shooting stars bring a wish so near.
Planets giggle in their orbits round,
While we gaze up, stars all around.

The milky way dances in a swirl,
With cosmic laughter, our minds unfurl.
A meteor's dash, a sudden fright,
Yet we can't help but burst with delight.

So here we are under skies so vast,
In this moment, we forget the past.
Join the laugh track in stellar flight,
As tweety birds sing us into night.

Island Vibes

On this island, where hearts go free,
We paddle a boat of joy, whee!
Surfer dudes with their sandy dreams,
Catch the waves, or so it seems.

Tuk-tuks scoot with a honk and a beep,
As market scents wake us from sleep.
Mangoes for breakfast, oh what a treat,
With crunchy crabs that dance to the beat.

Palm fronds wave like hands at play,
While children giggle, splashing in bay.
A grand fiesta with music so loud,
To dance like nobody's in the crowd.

Island vibes, contagious and bright,
Where every moment feels just right.
In this paradise, so wild and free,
Join the laughter and be with me!

www.ingramcontent.com/pod-product-compliance
Lightning Source LLC
Chambersburg PA
CBHW070304120526
44590CB00017B/2552